ISBN 0-85116-336 - X

DO NOT READ FURTHER WITHOUT
THE PERMISSION OF THE OWNER

NAME ____________________

ADDRESS ____________________

____

____

THE TOPPER BOOK

Printed and Published by D. C. THOMSON & CO., LTD., 185 Fleet Street, London EC4A 2HS.

THE
TEENY
TOPPERS

PARK
AW, C'MON AND PLAY WITH US, DAD.
NO. I'LL HAVE A NAP WHILE YOU LOT PLAY.
YAWN!
SHOVE!
DRAG!

ZZZZZZ
HUP AND OVER!
LEAP!
BOUND!

ZZZZ
PULL!
LET'S TRY A BIGGER FROG.

MUCH BETTER.
ALLEY-OOP!
LEAP!
PROPPED UP!

ON TO THE SLIDE, NOW.
BAH! THOSE BRATS PLAYIN' AROUND HERE MAKE MY NICE, NEAT PARK LOOK UNTIDY!

YERP!
MAYBE YOU'LL WANT TO GO HOME AFTER YOU LAND ON THIS LOT! CACKLE!
WHOOSH!
TOSS!

HEH! HEH!
OW!
OW!
OW!
PRICK!
PRICK!
PRICK!

PLOT!
PLUCK!
PLUCK!
PLUCK!

TIE!
LOOK UNDER THIS BUSH, MR PARKIE.
WOT'S THERE?

HAUL!
I DON'T SEE NUFFIN'!
LOOK CLOSER.

DAD AWAY!
WHOOSH!

LOOK A LOT CLOSER, MR PARKIE!
YEOW!
WHUMP!
PRANG!

ZZZZZZ
I THINK WE MADE OUR POINT! HEH!

TRICKY DICKY

HO- HUM! TIME TO CRACK MY BOILED EGG.
WATCH ME SURPRISE DAD WITH THIS TRICK ONE.

ERK! WHERE'S IT GOT TO?
TEE- HEE- HEE!
CLACK!
TODDLE!

THERE IT IS! A SMASHIN' YOLK! HAW! HAW!
BLATCH!
SPLUTCH!

I HOPE YOU HAVEN'T DONE ANYTHING TO MY EGG, DICKY.
WIPE!
BLEH!
TSK! AS IF I WOULD.

BUT—
YEEK!
SWELL!

HELP!
SSSS
BEAT!
DOWN, YOU BEAST!
CLATTER!
HOO! HOO! THAT'S MY EGGSPANDING JOKE!
WAAARGH! IT'S STILL GROWING!
AARGH! I'M STUCK!
'BYE! I'M OFF TO SCHOOL, NOW. CACKLE!

SOON—
I'VE HIDDEN JOKE EGGS ALL ROUND THE ROOM. I'LL HIDE AND WATCH WHAT HAPPENS! HEE! HEE!
COOKERY CLASS

SO—
I'LL JUST OPEN THE FRIDGE—YIKES!
HAR!
SPROING!

WAA! EGGSPLOSIONS EVERYWHERE!
BANG!
CRACK!

STAY BACK, GIRLS! THAT EGG IS ACTING STRANGELY.
GIGGLE!
TEACHER
WOBBLE!

HAR! HAR! IT'S A CROCKER!
MUMMY!
WHIRR!
SMASH!
YEEK! A C-C-CROCODILE!

THIS ONE'S EGGSTRA-SPECIAL! CACKLE!

IT'S AN EGGSHELL! HAW! HAW!
?
PHOOM!
SPLUTCH!
H- HOW?
ULK!

GRR! WHICH WICKED GIRL DID THAT?
CRACK!
BUMP!
NOT ME, MISS. I WAS JUST GOING TO BEAT AN EGG— OOPS!
YAARGH!

SO! TRICKY DICKY! IF ANYTHING'S GONNA GET BEATEN—IT'LL BE YOU!
ULP! I DIDN'T EGGSPECT THIS!

HERE, GIRLS! USE THESE ROTTEN EGGS LEFT OVER FROM LAST TERM.
WOW! THANKS, MISS!

NOW THE YOLK'S ON DICKY! HAR!
HO! HO!
SPLOT!
SPLATT!
YUGH! YEUCH! BLEUCHLE! BLERCH!

ALI'S BABA
THE BABE WITH THE INVISIBLE BODYGUARD
BABA'S VISITING HIS UNCLE'S FARM—
REMEMBER, BABA—YOU MUSTN'T CLIMB THE TREE TO GET APPLES—YOU'RE ONLY ALLOWED TO EAT THE ONES THAT FALL.
MUMPH!
NONE FALL. BABA GONNA HAVE TO MAKE 'EM FALL!
NUDGE!
AS I THOUGHT!
YIKE! HE'S GONNA HIT THE FARMHOUSE WINDOW!
BAH! STONE MISS!
GOT IT . . . OUCH!
ZOOM!
GOOD JOB BABA BRING CATAPULT—BABA SHOOT APPLE DOWN!
YIKE! HE HASN'T SEEN THE FARM CAT—SNOOZING UP THAT TREE!
C'MON, PUSS! SHIFT! OW! OUCH! YOW!
SPIT! SNARL!
BABA GETTING BETTER—BABA NEARLY HIT ONE THAT TIME!
AAAGH! I DON'T LIKE THE LOOK ON THAT GOAT'S FACE—OR WHERE HE'S LOOKING!
BABA FIND GOOD ROUND STONE FOR CATAPULT.
NO . . . THAT ONE NOT ROUND . . .
PHEW! PULLED IT ROUND JUST IN TIME!
WHAM!
OOH!
NICE GOAT HELP BABA GET APPLES, DAD.
. . . SORRY I HAD TO ' BUTT IN ON YOUR FUN THERE!
TWEET! TWEET!

SEND FOR KELLY AND HIS ASSISTANT CEDRIC IN THE JUMBO CASE

CRASH!
SUPA CARS LTD.
NO NEED TO BUY A CAR. JUST CHUCK BANANAS THROUGH THE WINDOW—ETHEL WILL FIND A WAY IN.

AND WE CAN DRIVE OUT— SATISFIED CUSTOMERS!
SUPA CARS LTD.

MEANWHILE—
I SUSPECT THERE'S A CONNECTION BETWEEN THESE LATEST ROBBERIES AND THE MISSING ELEPHANT.
BANANA SKINS, YOU MEAN?

IN ANOTHER PART OF TOWN—
OPEN UP YOUR VAN OR JUMBO WILL SQUASH YOU FLAT.
SECURITY
BETTER DO AS THEY SAY, GODFREY. I DON'T PLAY SQUASH!

JUST THEN—
IS THAT YOU, KELLY? HURRY! THERE GO THE CROOKS!
AFTER THEM, CEDRIC.

DRAT! THEY'RE FORDING THE STREAM.
TOO DEEP FOR US— AND NOT A BRIDGE IN SIGHT.

PRESENTLY—
WELL, MR KELLY, WE'VE GOT WHAT WE NEED TO TRAP THE ELEPHANT.
ZOO
KEEP A SHARP LOOK-OUT. AN ELEPHANT'S NOT EASY TO HIDE.
BANANAS

LISTEN! AN ELEPHANT TRUMPETING!
YOU'RE RIGHT! THIS IS OUR CHANCE.
TRUMPET♫

GOT IT!
TRUMPET!
ERK!

WHAT'S THE IDEA? YOU'VE BUSTED MY TRUMPET! I'M NOT ALLOWED TO PRACTISE INDOORS.

FARTHER ON—
LOOK! HERE COMES A JUMBO.
NO MISTAKE THIS TIME.

CHARGE!

WOW! IT'S A JUMBO-JET! WE'RE ON THE RUNWAY.

HMM! . . HELICOPTERS! I THINK WE'LL HIRE ONE, CEDRIC.

SO—
LOOK—THERE'S THE CAGE WE ORDERED, CEDRIC.

OUR 'COPTER AND THIS CAGE BAITED WITH BANANAS IS THE ANSWER TO SOLVING THIS CASE.

SOON—
LOOK! THERE GOES JUMBO, HELPING TO ROB A FUR WAREHOUSE! LOWER THE CAGE.
FUR WAREHOUSE

FURS
WHASSAT? BANANAS!
CLUNK!

TOSS!
ULK!
FURS
CRUMP!
OUCH!
WHO CARES ABOUT FURS—I'M FOR 'NANAS.

WELL, WELL! WHAT'S THIS—A COUPLE OF BANANA SPLITS? HO! HO!
CHOMP! CHOMP!

KELLY TO BASE . . . ELEPHANT CROOKS ARE WAITING TO BE PICKED UP AT THE FUR WAREHOUSE.

C'MON, ETHEL—WE'RE TAKING YOU BACK TO THE ZOO.

CRUMBS! CLOSED! WE'LL HAVE TO TAKE ETHEL HOME FOR THE NIGHT.
ZOO CLOSED UNTIL TOMORROW

BACK HOME—
I HOPE THE NEIGHBOURS DON'T COMPLAIN ABOUT US HAVING AN ELEPHANT IN THE GARDEN.
I DON'T SEE WHY THEY SHOULD. NEXT DOOR'S GOT GARDEN GNOMES.
'NANAS!

SUDDENLY—
CRASH!
EEK! GET OUT, YOU BIG FAT 'NANA SNATCHER!

PHEW! GASP! IT WON'T BUDGE. THIS IS OUR NEXT CASE, CEDRIC—HOW TO GET RID OF AN ELEPHANT!

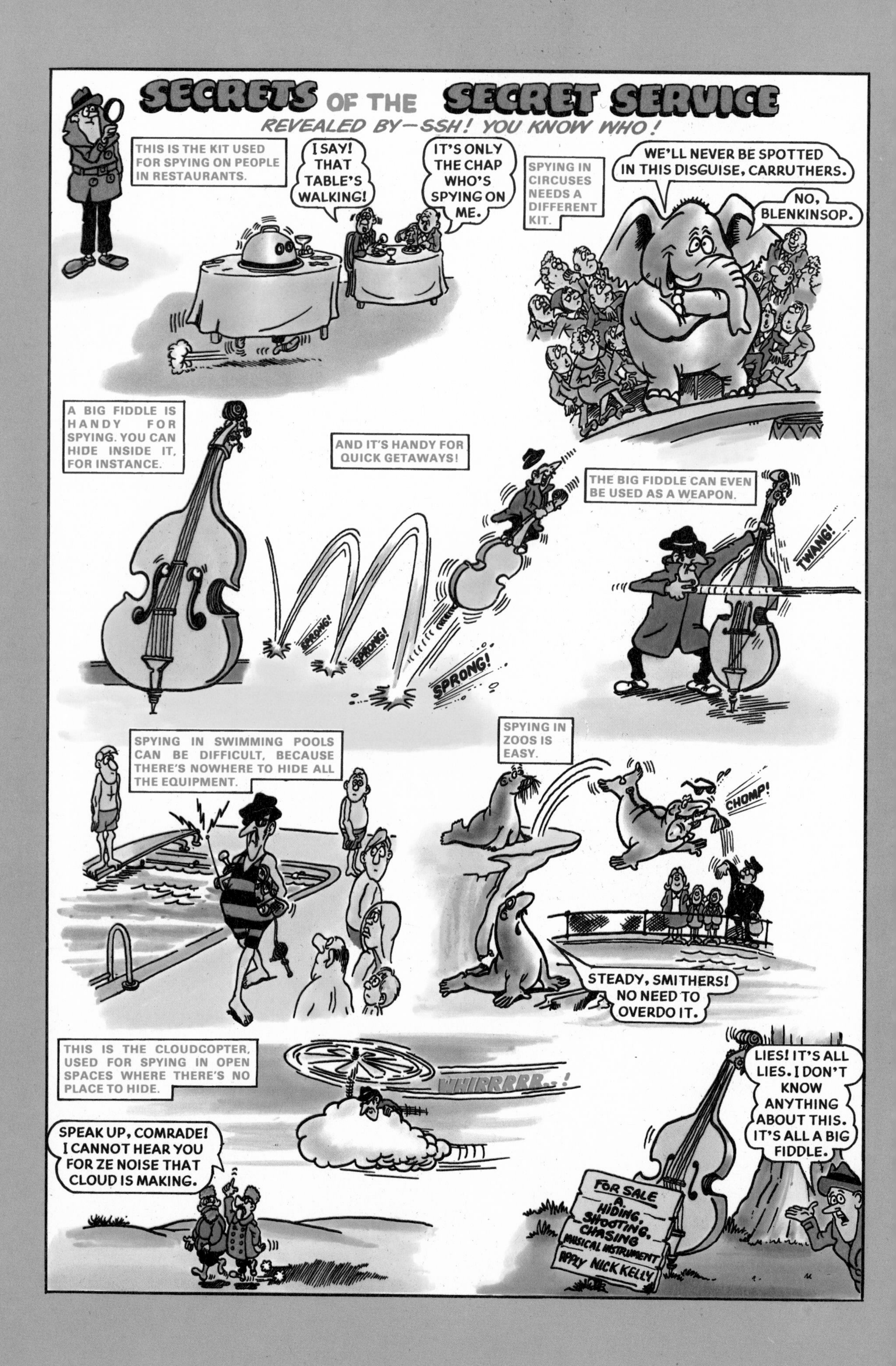
SECRETS OF THE SECRET SERVICE
REVEALED BY—SSH! YOU KNOW WHO!
THIS IS THE KIT USED FOR SPYING ON PEOPLE IN RESTAURANTS.
I SAY! THAT TABLE'S WALKING!
IT'S ONLY THE CHAP WHO'S SPYING ON ME.
SPYING IN CIRCUSES NEEDS A DIFFERENT KIT.
WE'LL NEVER BE SPOTTED IN THIS DISGUISE, CARRUTHERS.
NO, BLENKINSOP.
A BIG FIDDLE IS HANDY FOR SPYING. YOU CAN HIDE INSIDE IT, FOR INSTANCE.
AND IT'S HANDY FOR QUICK GETAWAYS!
SPRONG!
SPRONG!
SPRONG!
THE BIG FIDDLE CAN EVEN BE USED AS A WEAPON.
TWANG!
SPYING IN SWIMMING POOLS CAN BE DIFFICULT, BECAUSE THERE'S NOWHERE TO HIDE ALL THE EQUIPMENT.
SPYING IN ZOOS IS EASY.
CHOMP!
STEADY, SMITHERS! NO NEED TO OVERDO IT.
THIS IS THE CLOUDCOPTER, USED FOR SPYING IN OPEN SPACES WHERE THERE'S NO PLACE TO HIDE.
WHIRRRRRR...!
SPEAK UP, COMRADE! I CANNOT HEAR YOU FOR ZE NOISE THAT CLOUD IS MAKING.
LIES! IT'S ALL LIES. I DON'T KNOW ANYTHING ABOUT THIS. IT'S ALL A BIG FIDDLE.
FOR SALE A HIDING, SHOOTING, CHASING MUSICAL INSTRUMENT
APPLY NICK KELLY

DESERT ISLAND DICK
THE COMIC CASTAWAY

THIS BOOK ABOUT HYPNOTISM IS VERY GOOD, OLLY. I'LL TRY IT OUT ON YOU.
DICK'S OCTOPUS PAL.

LOOK INTO MY EYES . . . YOU ARE FEELING DROWSY!
GAZE!

NOW—JUMP UP AND DOWN LIKE A KANGAROO!

HEH! I'VE DONE IT!
STING!
ZZZ

ZZZ
KEEP JUMPING! THAT'S A GREAT BOOK!

WHUMP!

IT'S A GREAT BOOK, ALL RIGHT, DICK—IT THUMPED THAT WASP THAT MADE ME JUMP!
BLEH!

She's a sure-fire success—at perilousness!
BERYL the PERIL

DAD'S AT THE DOCTOR'S—
FEELING UNDER THE WEATHER, EH? PERHAPS YOU'VE BEEN LOSING YOUR TEMPER TOO OFTEN.
HUH! WITH A DAUGHTER LIKE BERYL, I CAN'T HELP IT.

BACK HOME—
THE DOCTOR SAYS I'VE BEEN LOSING MY TEMPER TOO OFTEN. I'VE GOT TO KEEP COOL.
POOR DAD!

THIS OPEN WINDOW WILL HELP YOU TO KEEP COOL, DAD.
SHUT THAT WINDOW, BERYL! BAH!
GUST!

PERHAPS WHAT YOU NEED IS SOME SOOTHING MUSIC.
SIGH! YES.

SO—
AGH! GO AWAY, YOU SILLY GIRL!
SKREEK! SCRAPE! SKREEEEEE!

OW!
OOPS! OH, WELL, MAYBE YOU WON'T BE ABLE TO HEAR ANY MUSIC NOW!
JAB!

STARTING TO BOIL OVER.
OH-OH! JUST AS WELL IT'S BEEN SNOWING.

HERE, DAD—A HANDFUL OF SNOW SHOULD HELP YOU KEEP COOL!
BRR-OW!

HERE, DAD—PUT YOUR FEET UP AND RELAX.
LIFT!

WHOOPS-A-DAISY! NOT A VERY SAFE CHAIR YOU'RE SITTING IN, IS IT?
WHUMP!

FUMING!
HANG ON, DAD . . .

HAVE SOME ICE-CUBES. THEY'LL HELP YOU TO KEEP COOL.

BOILING WITH RAGE!
NOW, NOW! WATCH THAT TEMPER! WHAT CAN I DO TO SOOTHE YOU?

I'LL DIM THE LIGHTS. THAT'S IT!

CRASH!
OW!
OOPS! A BIT TOO DIM, I THINK.

AND NOT VERY SOOTHING, EITHER, BY THE LOOKS OF THINGS!

SNARL! THAT DOES IT!
OOH!

HULLO, DOCTOR! I'M FEELING MUCH BETTER NOW.

GULP! BET I WON'T BE, IN A FEW MINUTES, THOUGH!

YOUNG Danny Wilson owns a super-marvellous transistor radio. With it, he can make objects larger, smaller, lighter than air or even invisible! However, the fantastic effects of the tranny's rays last for only a short time.

AND SHOULD YOU LOOK LIKE CRASHING ON THE WAY DOWN AGAIN—

—USE THE ENLARGING RAY—
GROWING RAY
LWS

—AND THAT SOLVES THE PROBLEM. HO! HO!

BUT, NEXT TRIP TO THE TOP OF THE HILL—
GEROFF!
HEY!

HE'LL BE SORRY HE TOOK MY SLEDGE.
I'LL LET YOU HAVE IT BACK WHEN I'M FINISHED—MAYBE! HO! HO!
FLOATING RAY
VMWV

SUDDENLY—
EEEK!
HO! HO!

I'M FALLING OFF! HELP!
OH, DEAR!

SHRINKING RAY
SW
I CAN'T LET HIM HURT HIMSELF.

EEK! I'M SHRINKING!

GOTCHA!
PHEW! SAVED!

LET THAT BE A LESSON TO YOU—OR I'LL DO SOMETHING WORSE NEXT TIME.
ER—YES! GULP!

BUT SUDDENLY, THE FLOATING RAY WEARS OFF THE SLEDGE—
CRUMP!
OUCH!
OH! I FORGOT ABOUT THAT!

IT'S TIME TO MAKE MYSELF SCARCE, I THINK! THAT'S EASY WHEN YOU'VE GOT A TRANNY LIKE MINE, EH?
GRR!
GROWING RAY
LW

QUAINT TALES

INTERESTING FOLK-TALES AND LEGENDS OF BRITAIN

A Scotsman called Donald McKay came across a wooden cask in a dark, Highland cave. Curious to find out what was inside, he bored a hole in it. A tiny figure popped out, and quickly grew to gigantic size. The figure asked Donald if he'd ever seen anything more amazing. Donald replied—" It would be more wonderful still if you could become tiny enough to enter the barrel again." So the figure quickly shrank and popped back inside. Donald immediately plugged the cask and ran for his life, never daring to return.

Once, a fierce dragon carrying a red-hot stone flew over Helston in Cornwall, seemingly all set to " bomb " the town. The townsfolk fled, but the dragon's aim must have been poor—the stone landed harmlessly on moorland half a mile away!

The Cornish Lord Pengerswick lived in luxury, thanks to the heavy taxes with which he burdened his people. One mid-summer he and some friends were feasting on board a ship drifting slowly with the tide near Cudden point. Without warning, the ship suddenly sank! Ever after, local fishermen said they could still hear laughter and singing coming from Pengerswick's banquet, still in full swing beneath the waves.

For years a fierce wyvern—a kind of dragon—terrorised Coed-y-Moch in Wales, killing men and animals. All attempts to slay it failed until a young lad called Meredyth found the beast in a deep sleep. Swinging his axe, Meredyth beheaded the beast with a single blow.

There is a story that a mysterious blacksmith worked in Wayland Smith's cave, near Ashbury, in ancient times. Anyone who wanted a horse shod had to go to the cave and place a coin on the anvil. Then, leaving the horse, they had to walk out of sight. On returning, the horse would be shod, but there would never be a sign of the smith.

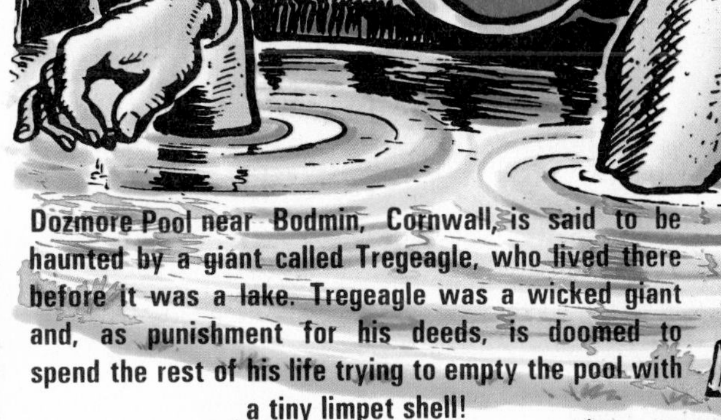

Dozmore Pool near Bodmin, Cornwall, is said to be haunted by a giant called Tregeagle, who lived there before it was a lake. Tregeagle was a wicked giant and, as punishment for his deeds, is doomed to spend the rest of his life trying to empty the pool with a tiny limpet shell!

At Kyleakin, in Skye, stands the ruins of Castle Maol, where a Norwegian princess is said to have once lived. She stretched a giant chain across the sound separating Skye from the mainland, and used to make passing ships or galleys pay a toll to her. When the toll was paid, the chain was lowered to allow the ship to proceed on its way.

An early 13th century legend tells of a merman, half fish, half man, who was captured by Suffolk fishermen. He was kept alive in a pool for six months, feeding on raw fish thrown to him by his captors. But at length he grew tired of this, and is believed to have escaped back to the open sea!

Beneath Bala Lake, in Wales, is said to lie the village of Old Bala. The story goes that, before there was a lake, the villagers appointed a man to put a cover over their well each night, believing some disaster would overtake them if this was not done. One night, the guardian forgot to put on the cover, and the well began to gush water. Nothing could stop it, and the villagers fled to the hills. By morning, the village was lost to sight beneath the waters of the lake.

F
I
WHERE'S FINGY, TOMMY?
DUNNO, MUM.
SUDDENLY—
WHAT ON EARTH'S GOING ON?
FINGY! STOP PLAYING ABOUT! HURRY AND GET DRIED.

FINGY RUSHES INTO ACTION—

—AND DEALS WITH THE FIRE FROTHWITH—ER—FORTHWITH!

WHAT A CLEVER FING! HOW CAN I REWARD HIM?
WELL, I TELL YOU WHAT . . .

N G Y
GO AND GET CLEANED UP, YOU MUCKY FING.
AND DON'T BE LONG. WE'RE BOTH DUE AT MABEL'S PARTY IN HALF AN HOUR.
SOON—
NOT LIKE THAT!
PEST! C'MON AND WE'LL GET OFF TO THAT PARTY NOW.
JUST THEN—
FIRE!
A SHAMPOO AND SET? NO PROBLEM. HE DID SAVE MY SHOP.
HO! HO!
AT MABEL'S PARTY—
HO! HO! IS THAT REALLY FINGY, TOMMY?
IT SURE IS! HE'S A PRETTY FING 'COS HE HAD A REAL POO— NOT A SHAMPOO!

One swig of his soup and Sidney Braithwaite becomes . . .

SOUPER BOY

I'LL FIX IT SO NOBODY'S HURT . . .
SMASH!
ZIP!
. . . SO THERE'S NO NEED TO PANIC . . .
CRASH!
YERK!
. . . JUST SIT BACK AND RELAX, GRANNY! . .
WAIL!
SOUPER-ZOOM!

. . . AND WATCH THIS!
AARGH!
WHUMP!

EH? WHAT'S UP? THAT'S THE SOFTEST CRASH- LANDING I'VE EVER MADE.
CATCH!
HAR! GOT IT!

NOW FOR A NICE QUIET CUPPA—EH, GRAN?
H-HALT!
SKID!

BUT...
YOU WICKED, WICKED BOY! LOOK AT THE MESS YOU'VE MADE OF THE AIRPORT! I'LL TEACH YOU TO BEHAVE YOURSELF!
VANDAL!
ERK! SORRY, GRANNY! I DIDN'T NOTICE. HELP!
SCOOT!

HUNGRY HORACE

FRED

I'LL HOP OVER THIS FACTORY WALL AN' BREAK IN.

OOF!
CRUMPLE!

WHAT'S GOIN' ON? THAT WALL'S JUST MADE OF CARDBOARD!

I'LL BASH IT DOWN! CHA-ARGE!
STAFF

YELK! A R-RUBBER D-DOOR?
BOUNCE!
STAFF

WHEEEE!
OOGH!
SPLASH!

AH! THERE'S THE SAFE! I'LL GRAB THE LOOT, AN' GERROUT O' HERE.
MANAGER
SAFE

THE
FLOP

LET'S SEE WHAT I CAN FIND IN HERE.
STAFF

YEEIPES!
PULLLLLL!

AHA! THERE'S AN OPEN WINDOW!
STAFF

SO—
OH, WELL, AT LEAST THE WINDOW'S NOT BOOBY-TRAPPED.
WELL, NOT THE WINDOW, FRED!
BZZT!

BIFF!
SPROING!

JOKE FACTORY
AGH! I SHOULD HAVE GUESSED!
IT'S ALL THANKS TO TRICKY DICKY. HE SET UP OUR BURGLAR-PROOF SYSTEM.

BADDIE

GOODIE

Mickey
THE
MONKEY

POLICE STATION
OH, DEAR! OH, DEAR! OH, DEAR!

ER, CHIEF CONSTABLE, SIR. I DON'T KNOW HOW TO TELL YOU THIS, BUT I . . . WELL, OUT IN THE STREET THERE . . .

. . . MY SHOE FELL OFF.

PARDON ME ONE MOMENT, SIR.
JERK!

ONE . . . TWO . . .

WELL, SIR. YOUR PROBLEM SEEMS TO BE OVER.
I GATHER FROM MY CLOSE INSPECTION THAT YOUR SHOE MUST HAVE FALLEN BACK ON AGAIN.

NO, IT DIDN'T. IT'S STILL OUT THERE AND IT'S A BIG PROBLEM, REALLY . . .
THIS IS A MYSTERY TOO DEEP FOR A MERE DESK- SERGEANT, WHO SHOULD BE AT HIS TEA- BREAK.

OOO, LUMME!
WOOF!

KINDLY COUNT THIS GENTLEMAN'S SHOES.
ONE . . . TWO!
ONE . . . TWO!
WOOF . . . WOOF!

THERE YOU ARE, SIR. A MASSIVE POLICE INVESTIGATION SHOWS THAT YOUR SHOE HAS NOT FALLEN OFF.

BUT IT HAS AND IT'S BROUGHT THE WHOLE TOWN TO A STANDSTILL!
ONE SHOE BROUGHT THE WHOLE TOWN TO A . . .

GASP!
POLICE STATION
THERE! LOCK ME AWAY. IT'S THE LAST TIME I'LL EVER DRIVE A LORRY IN THE CHARITIES PARADE, BELIEVE ME!
PEEP!
HURRY UP!
HONK!

NORTH POLE
PRESENT TESTING DEPT.
PROP. F. CHRISTMAS
BOOKS
GOING UP IN THE WORLD BY L.E. VATOR
ROLLER SKATES
100 Yo-Yo's
POLICE OUTFITS
SANTA SUITS
NURSE OUTFITS
DOCTOR OUTFITS
DO NOT DISTURB TILL DEC 24TH
RED PAINT
HORROR MASKS
TEDDY BEARS
BUILDING BRICKS
OTHER WAY UP, STUPID!
ELECTRONIC GAMES
MARBLES
CHEMIST'S Outfit

HERE'S A CHALLENGE FOR YOU AND YOUR PALS! STUDY THE PICTURE FOR ONE MINUTE, THEN GIVE IT TO A PAL. GET HIM OR HER TO ASK YOU TEN QUESTIONS ABOUT IT—THINGS LIKE, "HOW MANY REINDEER ARE IN THE PICTURE?" OR "WHAT MUSICAL INSTRUMENT IS THE GNOME ON THE RIGHT PLAYING?" AWARD YOURSELF ONE POINT FOR EACH CORRECT ANSWER, THEN SWAP OVER.
THE TITLE, "TOPPER MEMORY SUPERSTAR 1986" GOES TO THE HIGHEST SCORER!
SOCKS
SHOE
SANTA'S GROTTY
200 NURSE OUTFITS
200 RATMAN OUTFITS
200 "RATMAN" OUTFITS
PAINTING BY NUMBERS
PAINTING BY NUMBERS
WATER PISTOLS
PAINTING BY NUMBERS
SWEETS
YUM BAR
PLAY HOUSE
BALLOONS
DOLL'S CLOTHES
"FRACTION MAN" THE NEW COMPUTERISED DOLL FOR BOYS
MAGIC SET
MAGIC SET
DOCTOR'S OUTFIT
ASTRO
ASTRO BATTLE
FIRE
3000 SPACE INTRUDERS
HANDLE WITH CARE!

Things look lively when this lad's around!
PETER PIPER
REMEMBER TO WEED THE GARDEN, PETER. I DON'T WANT TO SEE ANY WEEDS WHEN I COME BACK.
SIGH! OKAY, DAD! CHEERIO!
THERE'S JUST THE MAN TO HELP ME CHOP DOWN THOSE WEEDS. I'LL BRING HIM TO LIFE WITH MY MAGIC PIPES.
SEE "JUNGLE JOE" AT THE XYZ CINEMA
HEY, JOE! WILL YOU HELP ME WITH SOME WEEDING?
NOT LIKELY. I'M GOING TO HATCH THIS EGG I'VE FOUND.
I'VE AN IDEA!
CARTOON FUN
OLIVE THE OSTRICH
OLIVE WILL HATCH YOUR EGG FOR YOU IF YOU HELP ME WEED THE GARDEN!
IT'S A DEAL!
IT'S ALL YOURS, OLIVE.
EEK!
WOW!
CRACK!
I SAY! IT'S A LESSER-SPOTTED CHOMPING LIZARD!

ERK! OUR HEDGE— RUINED!
CHOMP!

HOI!
RIP!
CHOMP!

I'LL GET THIS GAUCHO TO HELP!
GAUCHO JOE
EATS GREEN'S BEANS

I WEEL STOP EET WEETH MY BOLAS!
CHOMP!

CARAMBA! HE HAS CHOMPED EET!
CHOMP!

EXHIBITION OF MEDIAEVAL ARMOUR IN THE MUSEUM
THERE'S ONLY ONE THING FOR IT!

VERILY, YOU SHALL BREAK YOUR TEETH!
CRACK!

WHEW! THANK GOODNESS THAT'S DONE. TAKE HIM TO THE ZOO, SIR KNIGHT.

AH, PETER— NO WEEDS?
ER! NO, DAD!

NO GARDEN!

HOI! TERRY! WHY ARE YOU DRESSED AS AN INDIAN? YOU'RE SUPPOSED TO BE A COWBOY IN OUR GAME.
NO, I'M NOT! YOU ARE!
A CHALLENGE, THEN! THE LOUDEST INDIAN CALL WINS.
UM SURE! HERE GOES . . . AWOOAA!
OUT YOU GO! I'M NOT HAVING ALL THAT NOISE IN THE HOUSE!
LATER—
TRY AGAIN—WHOEVER SQUIRTS THE TARGET FIRST GETS TO BE THE INDIAN.
FAIR ENOUGH.
YIKES!
DROP!
BUMP!
WURGLE!
SPLOTCH!
TOM
and

YAH! YOUR CALL WAS RUBBISH! LISTEN TO THIS . . . AWOOAWOOA!
?
AWOOYAH!
HUH! BUTCH WINS!
WOO-HOO!
OOH! YOU ROTTER! YOU SABOTAGED MY PISTOL!
SPLOOSH!
OKAY, THEN—THE FARTHEST KICK WINS.
HUH! YOU'LL WIN EASILY.
BOOT!
HO! HO! THERE'S NO DOUBT ABOUT IT NOW, TOM—YOU'LL HAVE TO BE THE PAIL-FACE! HAW! HAW!
BLOORSH!
TERRY

Willie Walker and the WONDERFUL
WHIZZERS FROM OZZ
COUGH!
YOUR SORE THROAT WILL SOON BE BETTER, WILLIE, 'COS THE THREE OF US ARE GOING TO HAVE A SUPER-WHIZZ TIME BACK ON OZZ!
Willie Walker must be the luckiest boy on Earth. He has two chums called Krik and Krak—twins from the land of Whizz on far-off Planet Ozz! They come to visit him regularly. And sometimes they even take him off to Ozz on holiday!
LET'S SEE WHAT'S HAPPENING THERE JUST NOW . . . I'LL SWITCH ON THE OZZNEWS FILE.
I BROUGHT ALONG SOME COUGH-SWEETS.
HERE IS AN EMERGENCY ANNOUNCEMENT.
INFORMATION IS JUST COMING IN OF THE RAPID SPREAD OF AN UNKNOWN PLANT ORGANISM, WHICH . . .
GOLLY WHIZZ! WHAT'S HAPPENED TO THE ANNOUNCER?
I DON'T KNOW, KRIK, BUT WE'D BETTER GET BACK TO OZZ—FAST!

Suddenly, another face appeared on-screen—
IT'S MR NONO, OUR TEACHER!
URGENT, TO KRIK AND KRAK! DO NOT RETURN TO OZZ! REPEAT—DO NOT RETURN . . .

WHAT? WHY? OH, NO! THE SIGNAL'S BEEN LOST!

The twins' little space-car shot through deep space at the speed of light.
WE'RE HEADING FOR OZZ, WHATEVER NONO SAYS. WE MUST FIND OUT WHAT'S HAPPENING.
I WONDER IF IT'S GOT ANYTHING TO DO WITH THE NEWSREADER GOING ALL GREEN?
At length, the amazing Whizz-car was preparing to land at Whizzport One.
MR NONO'S WAITING FOR US!
DON'T LAND, BOYS! DON'T LAND!
Mr Nono, his attention on the Whizz-car, had not yet seen a strange-looking vegetable-like creature moving up behind him.
Without warning, the creature—a creature that had once been an Ozz dog—brushed against Mr Nono—
—and a startling transformation began to take place!
N . . . URGH!
Soon, Mr Nono was unrecognisable, looking almost like a giant vegetable!
THAT'S WHAT THE NEWSREADER LOOKED LIKE! LET'S HEAD FOR THE OZZPUTER CENTRE. IT SHOULD TELL US WHAT'S GOING ON.

At the Ozzputer Centre—
MORE PLANT PEOPLE! D'YOU THINK THEY'RE ALL PEOPLE WHO HAVE BEEN CHANGED, SOMEHOW, LIKE MR NONO?
THE MULTI-OZZBOT WHO CONTROLS THE COMPUTER WILL TELL US.
OZZPUTER CEN

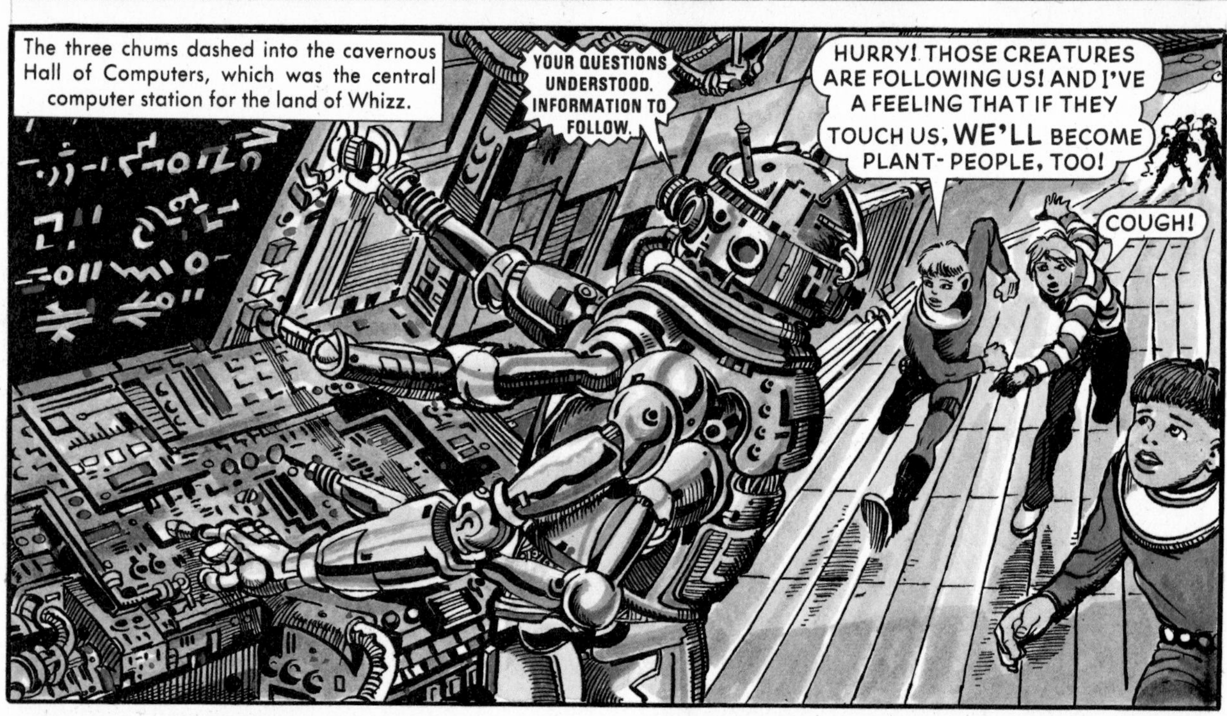
The three chums dashed into the cavernous Hall of Computers, which was the central computer station for the land of Whizz.
YOUR QUESTIONS UNDERSTOOD. INFORMATION TO FOLLOW.
HURRY! THOSE CREATURES ARE FOLLOWING US! AND I'VE A FEELING THAT IF THEY TOUCH US, WE'LL BECOME PLANT-PEOPLE, TOO!
COUGH!

Krak pulled out an odd-shaped gun, and dialled a certain code.
OUR WHIZZ-PISTOL'S FREEZO-RAY SHOULD STOP THEM MOVING FOR A BIT.
ALL THE INFORMATION CONCERNING THE "PLANT PEOPLE" INDICATES THAT A VEGETABLE SPORE FROM OUTER SPACE INFECTED AN OZZ INHABITANT AND THE INFECTION IS NOW BEING PASSED ON BY TOUCH, AND . . .
WHAT'S THAT NOISE?

The plant-people had broken free of the ice!
GULP! THEY'VE GOT TO BE STOPPED . . .
I OBEY!
The multi-ozzbot clanked into action!
I OBEY!
GOSH! THE OZZBOT HEARD WHAT I SAID!
I OBEY!
TO THE SPACE-CAR! LET'S GO-GO-GO!
But, at the doorway—
MORE OF 'EM!
SOCKO-FISTS ON!
AND WRIST-SHIELDS!

From the Whizzers' wrist-bands sprang rapidly-inflating "rubber balls" and expanding circles of metal!
HAVE A SOCKO-FIST!
DON'T LET THEM TOUCH US!
But, outside—
THEY'RE EVEN IN THE SPACE CAR! SCATTER —THEY MUSTN'T GET US TOGETHER!
KRIK! RADIO CONTROL!
OF COURSE!
Krik punched another wrist control, and—
THE RADIO-CONTROLLED TAKE-OFF'S GOT RID OF THEM.
PISTOLS AT KZXIO AND MAKE FOR THE CAR.
Meanwhile, Willie was still in trouble—
COUGH! GASP! I RECKON PLANTS CAN'T SWIM, SO I SHOULD BE SAFE ON THE OTHER SIDE.

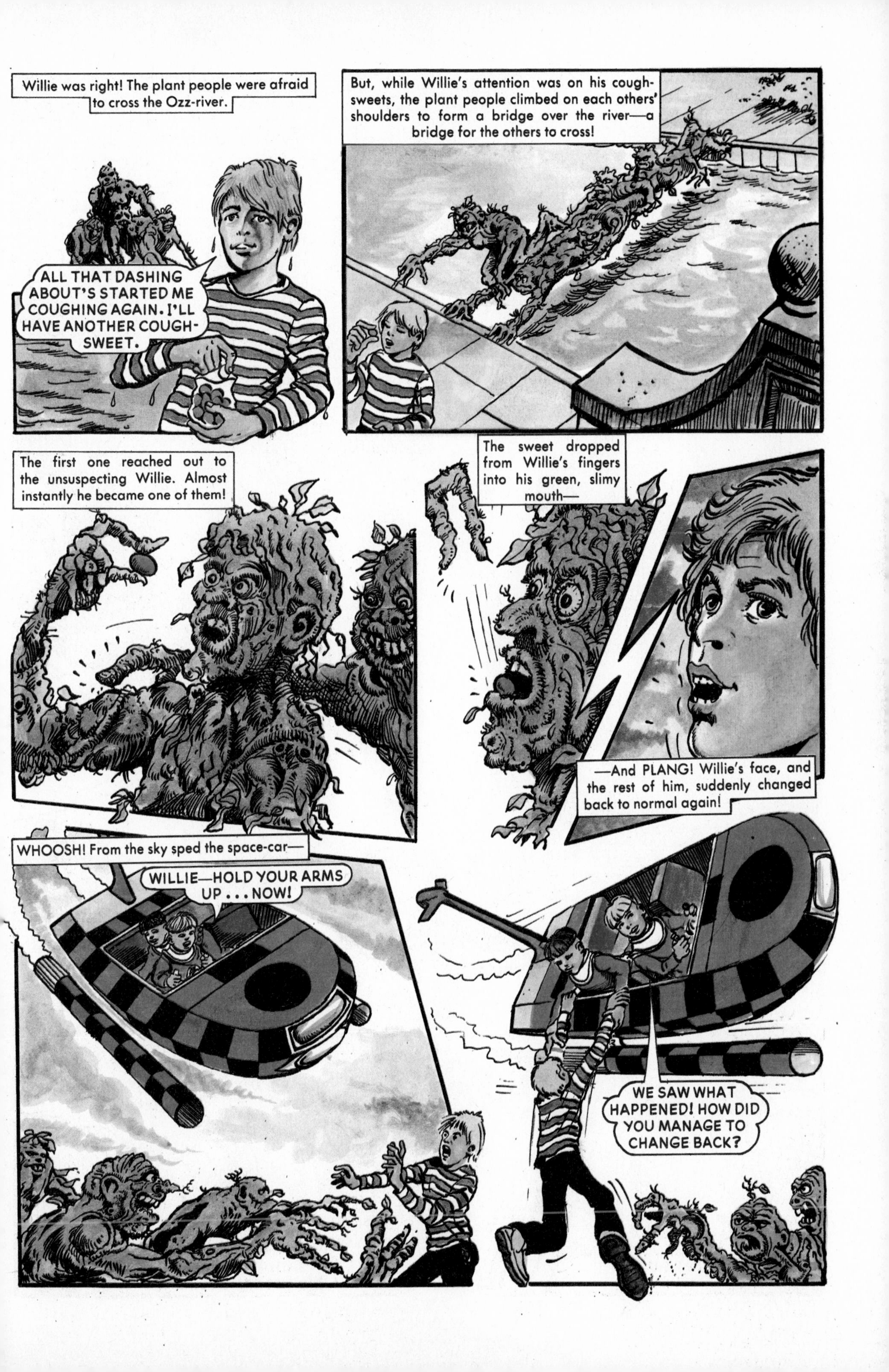
Willie was right! The plant people were afraid to cross the Ozz-river.
ALL THAT DASHING ABOUT'S STARTED ME COUGHING AGAIN. I'LL HAVE ANOTHER COUGH-SWEET.
But, while Willie's attention was on his cough-sweets, the plant people climbed on each others' shoulders to form a bridge over the river—a bridge for the others to cross!
The first one reached out to the unsuspecting Willie. Almost instantly he became one of them!
The sweet dropped from Willie's fingers into his green, slimy mouth—
—And PLANG! Willie's face, and the rest of him, suddenly changed back to normal again!
WHOOSH! From the sky sped the space-car—
WILLIE—HOLD YOUR ARMS UP . . . NOW!
WE SAW WHAT HAPPENED! HOW DID YOU MANAGE TO CHANGE BACK?

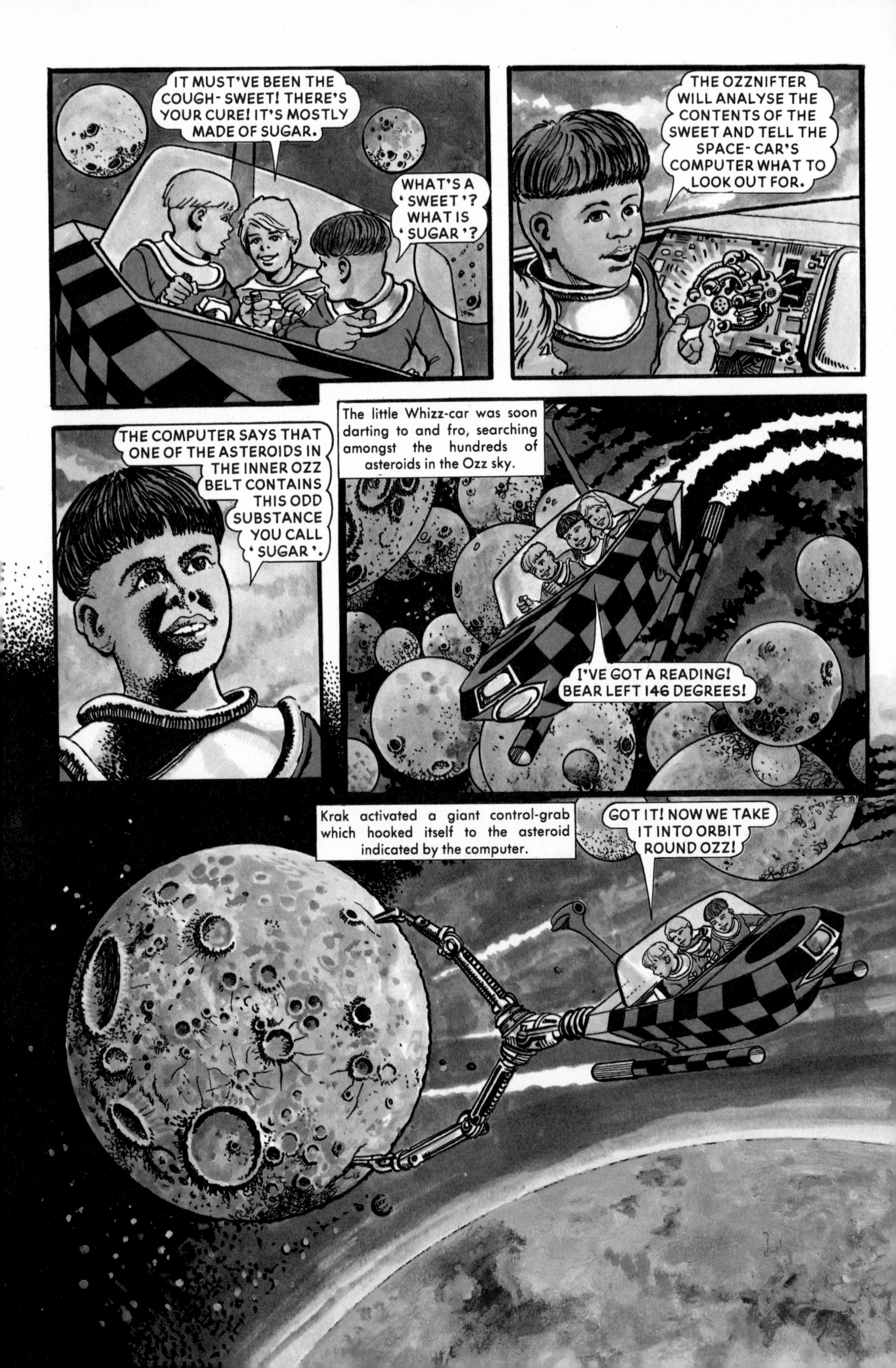
IT MUST'VE BEEN THE COUGH-SWEET! THERE'S YOUR CURE! IT'S MOSTLY MADE OF SUGAR.
WHAT'S A 'SWEET'? WHAT IS 'SUGAR'?
THE OZZNIFTER WILL ANALYSE THE CONTENTS OF THE SWEET AND TELL THE SPACE-CAR'S COMPUTER WHAT TO LOOK OUT FOR.
THE COMPUTER SAYS THAT ONE OF THE ASTEROIDS IN THE INNER OZZ BELT CONTAINS THIS ODD SUBSTANCE YOU CALL 'SUGAR'.
The little Whizz-car was soon darting to and fro, searching amongst the hundreds of asteroids in the Ozz sky.
I'VE GOT A READING! BEAR LEFT 146 DEGREES!
Krak activated a giant control-grab which hooked itself to the asteroid indicated by the computer.
GOT IT! NOW WE TAKE IT INTO ORBIT ROUND OZZ!

Several miles above Planet Ozz, the twins released the asteroid. Then, pulling back to a safe distance . . .
FIRE! DIRECT HIT! THE WINDS SHOULD SPREAD THE SUGAR ANTIDOTE ALL OVER THE PLANET!
Sure enough, as the sugar in the air spread over the planet . . .
A MIRACLE! WE'RE CURED!
WE'RE TURNING BACK TO NORMAL!
AN AMAZING SUBSTANCE, THIS SHOOGR.
YOU MEAN SUGAR? WELL, DENTISTS ON EARTH WOULDN'T AGREE!
All too soon, it was time for Willie to return to Earth—
'BYE!
Not long after, in Willie's house back on Earth—
CARE TO STAY FOR TEA, BOYS? I'M MAKING A LOVELY SALAD, WITH PEAS, LETTUCE . . .
GROOH! GREENERY? ER . . . NO, THANKS!

AL CHANGE
MASTER OF DISGUISE

EARLY ONE MORNING (JUST AS THE SUN WAS RISING)—
OI! LESS NOISE, DOWN THERE! I'M TRYING TO SLEEP.
WOT?
RATTLE!

BELT UP, AN' STICK SOME OF THIS SMELLY STUFF IN YER EARS!
SQUIRT!
BLOP!
NOT VERY FRESH YOGHURT

ONE CLEAN-UP JOB LATER—
THIS MEANS WAR!
DISGUISES

NEXT MORNING—
WHOO'S DISTURBING MY BEAUTY SLEEP?
DINKLE-DONKLE-YEEK!
SHOCK!
SQUIRT!
ANCIENT CREAM
RATTLE!
RATTLE!

PLUMMET!
SLIP!
THIS BRANCH IS SLIPP...EEH!
WHOMP!

STOOPID OVERGROWN BUDGIE!
I NEED ANOTHER IDEA.
FLAP!
FLAP!
LIMP!
HA!
HA!

IN AL'S DRESSING-ROOM—
I'M NOT FINISHED YET, FOLKS!
POGO STICK

AL CHANGE'S
MYSTERY MESSAGE

WHAT'S WRONG WITH AL?
HO- HUM!

2+2=$4

BUZZ!
BUZZ!

WHAT AM I DOING?

PEEP!

FORE!

BAAH! BLEAT!

HIYA, TWIN!

LET ME SHOW YOU, READERS.
USING DISGUISES, OF COURSE!
CAW! CAW!
THIS AGAIN, FOLKS!
PHEW! THIS IS A BIG ONE!
WHAT'S THIS?
SATURDAY 21st
SATURDAY 21st
GOT IT, YET? WELL, HERE'S THE ANSWER—IF YOU HAVEN'T ALREADY WORKED IT OUT.
EYE HAM BOARD BEE CAWS EYE CAN KNOT THINK OFF N KNEE FING FORE EWE TWO DAY.
TRANSLATION: I AM BORED BECAUSE I CANNOT THINK OF ANYTHING FOR YOU TODAY!

The Teeny Toppers
THERE Y'GO, TORTY.
YA! SLOWCOACH!
TA.
BERTRAM, THE BULLY NEXT DOOR AND HIS PET FERRET.
ALPHONSE
SERVES YOU RIGHT, SILLY BEAST!
POOR OL' TORTY'S GETTING COLD!
EECH! I'M STUCK!
BRR!
STRUGGLE!
SHIVER!
SHIVER!
PLOT!
OUT, SQUATTER!
I'M TRYIN'!

WAARGH!
GRAB!
TOPPLE!
EECH!
YOU JOIN HIM!
BOOT!

WHAT ARE YOU UP TO, BERTRAM?
ERK! MUM!
FILTHY!
GRUBBY!
DIRTY!

GO GETTIM, ALPHONSE!
HEY!
EECH! I'LL SPEED YOU UP, PAL!
YEOW!
BITE!
OOH, THE PAIN!
PLOP!
ZIP!
RING-A-RING-O'-ROSES . . .
EH?
HAUL!
. . . YOU FALL DOWN!
ERP!
SHOVE!

SAVE ME! IF MUM SEES ME WITH HER WASHIN' ALL BLACK . . .
WE COULD HELP.

WHAT A MESS! WHERE IS THAT BOY?
CHUCKLE!
GOOD TORTOISE IMITATION, BERTRAM!
CRAWL!
G-GULP!
EECH! TIME TO HIDE!

Danny's Tran y
GROWING RAY
LW
FLOATING RAY
MW
SHRINKING RAY
SW
VANISHING RAY
VHF
CLICK!
CLICK!
CLICK!
CLICK!

THIS IS JUST A TRAINING SESSION, DANNY. COME BACK IN THE AFTERNOON FOR THE REAL THING.
I WILL, UNCLE MARKO.

SUDDENLY—
CRACK!
HELP!

HE'LL BREAK HIS NECK!
EEH!
I'LL SAVE HIM, UNCLE—THE SAME WAY I SAVED THAT BULLY ON MY SLEDGE.

HO! HO! COME TO NICO, TONI!
CATCH ME!

PHEW! THANKS TO YOU, DANNY, I'VE ONLY GOT A TWISTED ANKLE INSTEAD OF A BROKEN NECK. I'LL HAVE TO MISS A PERFORMANCE OR TWO—BUT ZENA, HERE, CAN TAKE MY PLACE.
BACK TO NORMAL AGAIN
BAH! I'M BETTER THAN ZENA. I SHOULD GET THE CHANCE TO STAR.

THAT AFTERNOON—
GOOD LUCK, ZENA.
THANKS, DANNY.
HEH! SHE'LL NEED MORE THAN LUCK! AND WITH HER OUT OF THE WAY, I'LL HAVE MY CHANCE.

HERE I GO!
THEN—
TWANG!
THE TIGHTROPE'S SNAPPED.
QUICK AS A FLASH DANNY AIMED HIS TRANNY—
HOORAY!
FLOATING RAY
TCH! THAT BRAT'S INTERFERED AGAIN.
COO! SHE'S WALKING ON AIR.

LATER, BEFORE THE EVENING PERFORMANCE BEGAN—
TICKETS
I'VE PUT OIL ON THE TRAPEZE! IT'S GOOD-BYE ZENA— HER LAST PERFORMANCE!

SOON—
WISH ME LUCK AGAIN, DANNY!
YOU NEED IT, ZENA. I THINK SOMEONE'S TRYING TO SABOTAGE YOUR ACT.

IF I PUT ON A REALLY GREAT SHOW I'LL MAYBE GET MY OWN ACT AFTER TONI COMES BACK.

EEEH! THE BAR'S GREASY!

OH! ZENA'S FALLING.
SAVE HER.

BUT ONCE MORE DANNY WAS ON HAND!
GROWING RAY
LWS
THE AUDIENCE THINK IT'S PART OF THE ACT, THANK GOODNESS.

LATE THAT NIGHT, DANNY TOOK UP A SECRET HIDING-PLACE IN THE BIG TOP . .
I'M POSITIVE SOMEONE'S FIXING THOSE ACCIDENTS. SO LET'S SEE IF I CAN TRAP THE VILLAIN.

SURE ENOUGH, SOON . . .
AHA! SOMEONE WITH WIRE-CUTTERS— ALL SET FOR MORE SABOTAGE!

VANISHING RAY
W VHF
RIGHT, DUMBO! FIRE!
EH?

ARGH!
SCOOSH!
HO! HO!

HELP!
WELL DONE, DUMBO! HE COULDN'T SEE YOU—'COS YOU WERE INVISIBLE!

GREAT WORK, DANNY! THAT SCOUNDREL'S NASTY STUNTS MIGHT HAVE WORKED, IF IT HADN'T BEEN FOR YOU.
NO PROBLEM, ZENA! AND I HOPE THINGS GO WITH A SWING TOMORROW.
GROWING RAY
LW S
OUCH!
PO
ALLOW ME TO GIVE YOU THE BIG BOOT, CHUM!

SQUARE EYES
JACK O'NORY
SPORTSMAN
THE T.V. FAN
OOPS! HOPE WE DIDN'T INTERFERE WITH YOUR TELLY-WATCHING, JACK.
BONK!
MINI TV.
NOTHING DOES THAT!
TACKLE!
WHY DON'T YOU JOIN IN OUR FRIENDLY GAME?
SQUELCH!
NO, TA! I'M HAPPY ON THE BENCH! HEH!
GAZE
PUFF!
COMING ON A TRAINING RUN, JACK?
SPLASH!
YOUTH CLUB COACH
I'M HAPPY RUNNING MY EYES OVER THE TELLY!
PANT!

IT'S GREAT IN OUR BOXING CLUB, JACK.
I'VE GOT MY OWN 'BOX!' CHUCKLE!
SHADOW-BOXING
JACK NEVER DOES ANYTHING SPORTY.

BUT, SUDDENLY—
GAPE
WOW! LOOK AT JACK GO!
GAWK
ZOOM!

GOOD GRIEF! WHAT A LONG JUMP!
UMF!
SUPERB LEAP!
BLATT!

UGH!
FANTASTIC RUGGER TACKLE, JACK!
DIVE!
CRUMP!
OORFT!

EEEEYAH!
WHIRL!
GASP!
SWING!
← BOXING CHAPS →

DID YOU SEE THAT RIGHT UPPERCUT? WHAT A BOXER!
NING!
SOK!

GIVE!
WHINE! NO MORE! I'M SORRY!
HO! HO! ALL BECAUSE BULLY BOYLE PINCHED JACK'S TELLY!

YUP! JACK'S AN ALL-ROUND ATHLETE! BUT HE LEARNS IT FROM THE TELLY! HO! HO!
HEH! NO ONE PINCHES MY TELLY!
HERE AT SPORTS TIME . . .
HO! HO! HO!

WHISTLER
AND HIS
DOG

OH, LOOK! IT'S SNOWING! I WON'T BE ABLE TO GO TO SCHOOL TODAY, MUM.
RUBBISH, WHISTLER. BONZO WILL GET YOU THERE.
WHISTLER'S ELECTRONIC DOG, BONZO, IS FITTED WITH ALL SORTS OF GADGETS AND IS PROGRAMMED TO OBEY DIFFERENT SIGNALS FROM WHISTLER'S SPECIAL WHISTLE.

I COULD DO WITHOUT YOUR HELP SOMETIMES, BONZO.

CAN YOU HELP ME CLEAR THE SNOW OFF MY CAR, WHISTLER?
BONZO CAN.

AIR-BLAST ON, BONZO!
BLAST!
GREAT!

BUT—
OH!
STOP
HOO-HOO! BONZO BLEW THE SNOW OVER THOSE PEOPLE.

GRR!
BRAT!
PEST!
BUS STOP
S-SORRY!

I'LL GIVE YOU ALL A BLAST OF HOT AIR, FOLKS.
WARM BLAST!
HELP!
BUS STOP
AGH! TOO STRONG!
YIKES!

HE'S BLOWN THE CLOTHES CLEAN OFF US.
BRR!
GRR!
BUS STOP
LET'S GO. WE'RE IN HOT WATER.
STEADY, BONZO—HILL AHEAD.
AND IT'S TIME TO USE YOUR RUNNERS NOW.
OH, CRIKEY! WE'RE OUT OF CONTROL.
GOSH, WHISTLER, THAT'S A GREAT SLOPE FOR SLEDGING DOWN.
YEAH! BUT WE'VE GOT TO GO TO SCHOOL, UNLESS...
LATER, IN SCHOOL—
LOOK, SIR! A BLIZZARD.
YES! YOU'D ALL BETTER GO HOME BEFORE WE GET SNOWED UP. CLASS, DISMISS.
HO! HO! IT WAS A BONZO TRICK.
LET'S GO SLEDGING.
GOOD OLD BONZO.
AND SO—
YIPPEE!
HO! HO! EVEN TEACHER'S JOINED IN THE FUN.
WELL, IF YOU CAN'T BEAT 'EM, JOIN 'EM!

DESERT
ISLAND
DICK

EEK! THOSE BLOOMIN' BATS AGAIN!

I CAN'T GET A DECENT NIGHT'S SLEEP, IT'S SO CREEPY HERE!

GOSH! THAT LOOKS LIKE A KENNEL, OLLY!

I WISH WE HAD A FIERCE WATCHDOG TO PROTECT US FROM BATS AND THINGS.

HUH! NOT MUCH CHANCE OF GETTING A WATCHDOG HERE, THOUGH.
HMM! WE'LL SEE ABOUT THAT!

LATER—
HO! HO! WELL DONE, OLLY! WE'LL HAVE A SOUND SLEEP TONIGHT!

KEEP AWAY FROM THE ISLAND, LADS—THERE'S SOME KIND OF WATCHDOG GUARDING THE PLACE!
BARK! BARK!
ARF! ARF! I'M A WALRUS, REALLY—BUT I LIKE BEING A WATCHDOG!

A FUNTASTIC STORY
BY OUR BIGGEST STORY-TELLER
AH, BRITAIN AT LAST. IT'S A LONG WAY TO SWIM FROM DICK'S ISLAND!
WHAT'S THIS? POOR CHAP. I MUST DO SOMETHING!
PLEASE RESCUE ME! Desert Island Dick
AND HE DOES . . .
SOCIETY FOR THE RESCUE OF DESERT ISLAND DICK
GIVE GENEROUSLY
HUH! I DIDN'T GET MUCH. ONLY ENOUGH TO BUY A PICK AND SHOVEL.
NEVER MIND. I'LL DIG A TUNNEL TO THE ISLAND AND RESCUE HIM THAT WAY.
HOPE I'M NOT COMING UP TOO SOON OR THE WHOLE PACIFIC OCEAN WILL COME DOWN THIS HOLE.
WHOOPS! HOW RIGHT HE WAS!
WHOOSH!
THE PACIFIC OCEAN COMES BACK ALONG THE TUNNEL AND SWAMPS BRITAIN!
HELP!
GLUG!
GLUG! GLUG!
SOCIETY FOR THE RESCUE OF DESERT MOUNTAIN DICK
WHATEVER HAPPENED TO THE PACIFIC OCEAN?

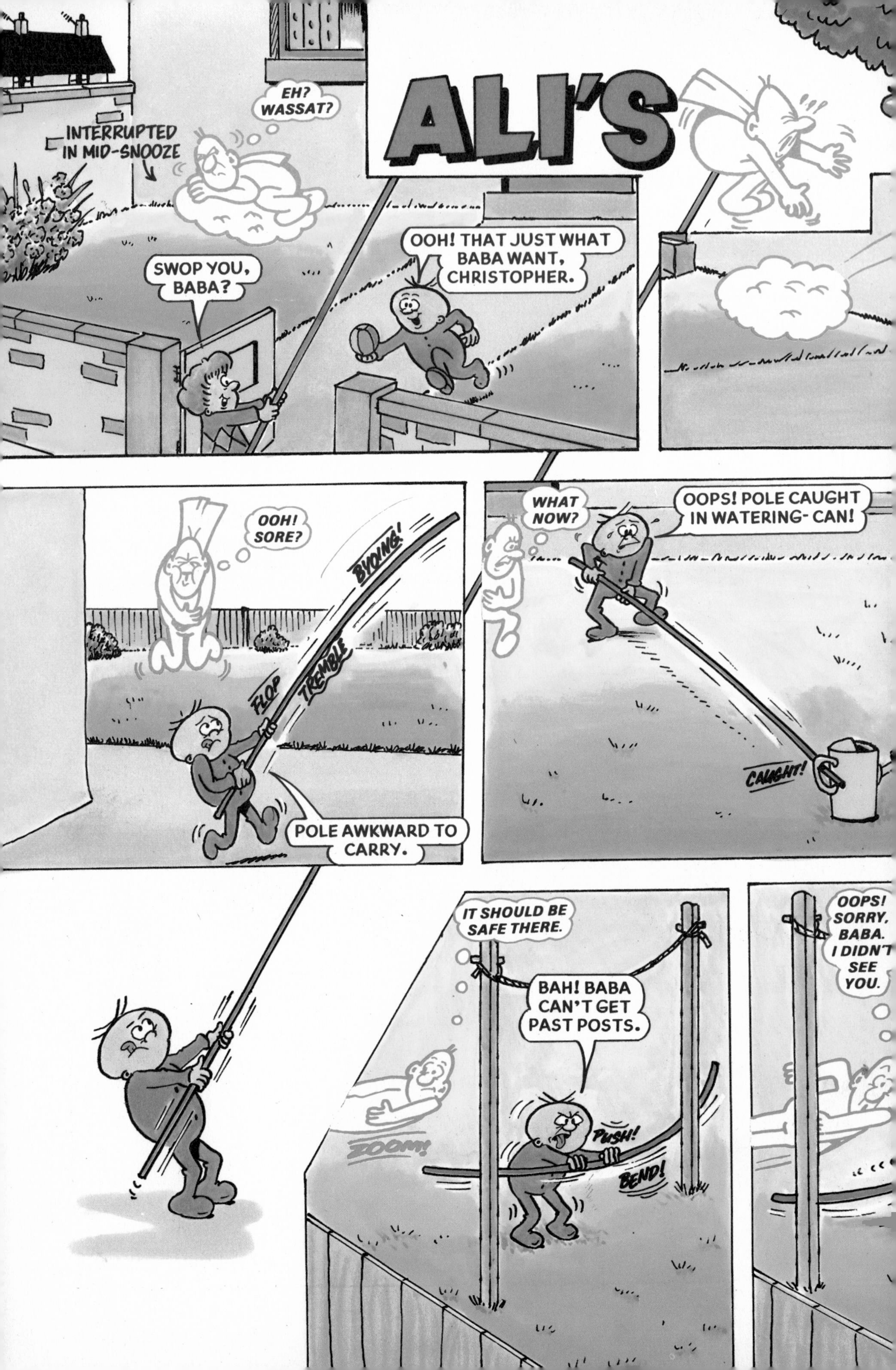
ALI'S
INTERRUPTED IN MID-SNOOZE
EH? WASSAT?
SWOP YOU, BABA?
OOH! THAT JUST WHAT BABA WANT, CHRISTOPHER.
OOH! SORE?
BYOING!
TREMBLE
FLOP
POLE AWKWARD TO CARRY.
WHAT NOW?
OOPS! POLE CAUGHT IN WATERING- CAN!
CAUGHT!
IT SHOULD BE SAFE THERE.
BAH! BABA CAN'T GET PAST POSTS.
ZOOM!
PUSH!
BEND!
OOPS! SORRY, BABA. I DIDN'T SEE YOU.

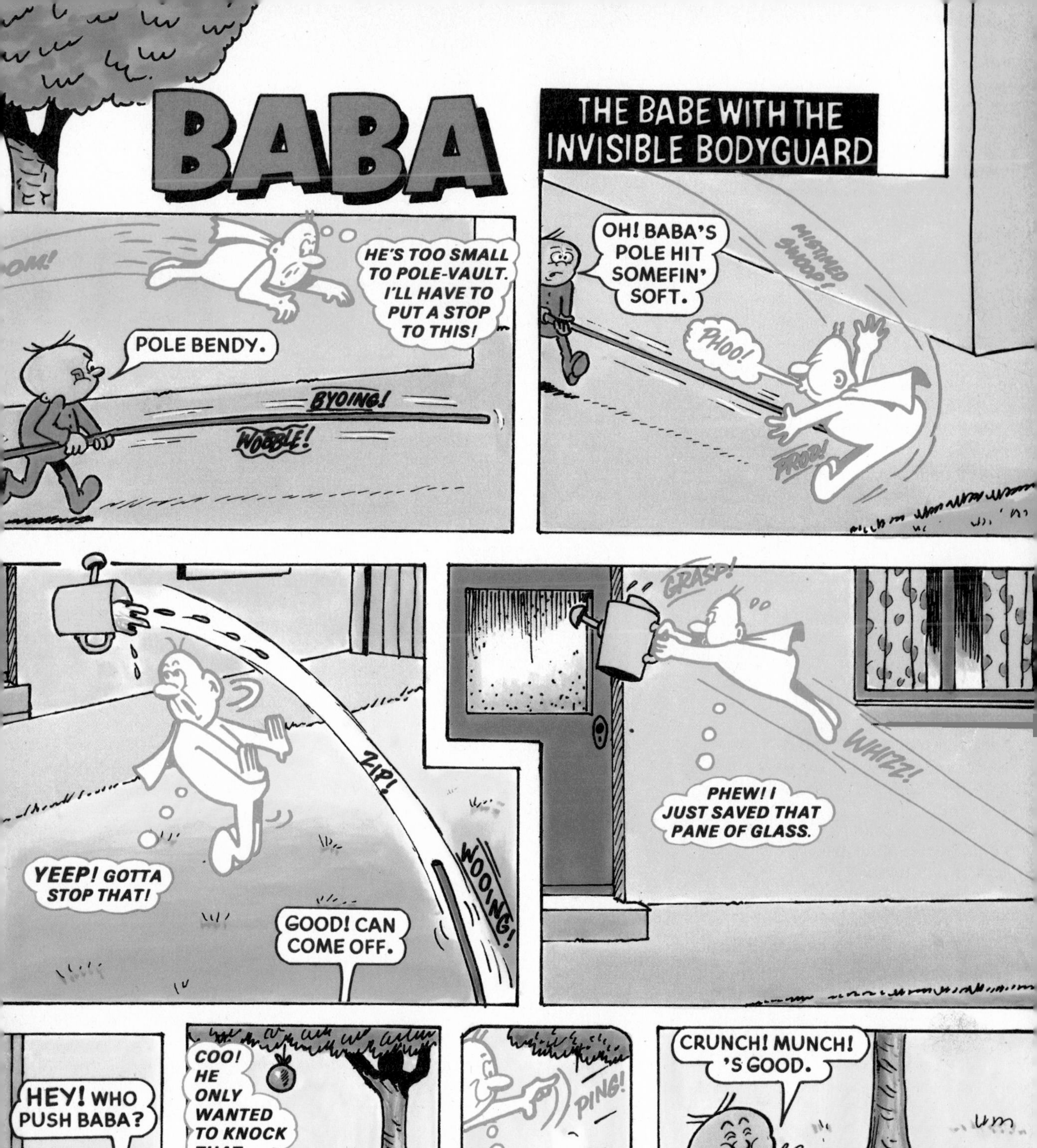
BABA
THE BABE WITH THE INVISIBLE BODYGUARD
HE'S TOO SMALL TO POLE-VAULT. I'LL HAVE TO PUT A STOP TO THIS!
POLE BENDY.
BYOING!
WOBBLE!
OH! BABA'S POLE HIT SOMEFIN' SOFT.
MISTIMED SWOOP!
PHOO!
PROD!
ZIP!
YEEP! GOTTA STOP THAT!
GOOD! CAN COME OFF.
WOOING!
GRASP!
WHIZZ!
PHEW! I JUST SAVED THAT PANE OF GLASS.

HEY! WHO PUSH BABA?
SNAP!
COO! HE ONLY WANTED TO KNOCK THAT APPLE DOWN.
SNIFF! CAN'T GET LAST APPLE DAD PROMISED BABA, NOW.

PING!
THERE Y'GO.
DROP!
YIPPEE! APPLE FALL DOWN BY ITSELF!

CRUNCH! MUNCH! 'S GOOD.
AW, SHUCKS! YOU'RE JUST THE APPLE OF MY EYE!

SEND FOR
KELLY
and his assistant
CEDRIC
in the case of the
ABOMINABLE
SNOWMEN

A WEEK'S SKIING HOLIDAY HERE WILL DO US A LOT OF GOOD, MR KELLY.
PLOP!
ULK!
YES—GOOD GRIEF! WHAT'S GOING ON OVER THERE?

PAH! THOSE PESKY YETI GOT MY WALLET.
YETI?
YEAH! ABOMINABLE SNOWMEN—RUNNIN' RIOT.

LATER—
I'LL MAKE THIS MY LAST RUN, THEN HAVE DINNER.

SUDDENLY—
TRIP!
YIKES!

GET YOUR THIEVIN' PAWS OFF MY WALLET! UGH!
SNATCH!

YETI! TWO OF 'EM. THE BLIGHTERS HAVE TAKEN MY MUNCHY BARS, AS WELL.

I'VE BEEN ROBBED BY TWO YETI.
ANOTHER ROBBERY!
THIS IS ALL VERY ODD, CEDRIC.

LATER—
YODEL-DEE-DEE! YODEL-DEE-DEE!

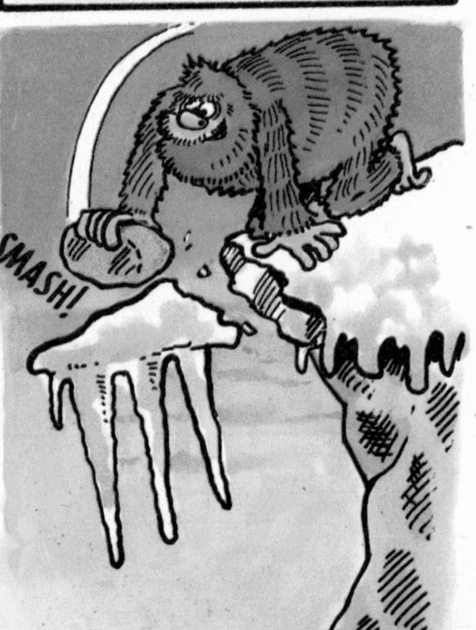
SMASH!

URK!
ZONK!

UR! UR!

WHAT HAPPENED?
YETI! ROBBED! DOH!

CEDRIC, IT'S UP TO US TO UNRAVEL THIS YETI MYSTERY.

SO—
WE KNOW THOSE YETI STEAL WALLETS—AND MUNCHY BARS—SO WE'LL SET A TRAP WITH MUNCHY BARS.
HO! THEY'LL GO FOR THE BARS AND SLIP INTO THE NET.

LET'S HIDE AND WAIT.

SOON—
LOOK, MR KELLY!
WHY, THE CRAFTY YETI!

OH, NO, YOU DON'T!

OH! WHAT AM I DOING?

SLIP!
SILLY ME!

CAREFUL, MR KELLY.
DON'T JUST STAND THERE. HELP ME OUT!

LET'S GO BACK TO THE VILLAGE. WE'LL HAVE TO THINK OF ANOTHER WAY.
WHAT'S THIS? A CRAFTY SIGN-SWITCH BY THE YETI!
DANGER
TWIST!

DANGER
IT'S LUCKY WE SAW THAT NOTICE.
YES. THIS MUST BE THE SAFE ROUTE.

OH, MR KELLY.
OH, CEDRIC!

A FINE HOLIDAY THIS IS TURNING OUT TO BE!
WHY DIDN'T WE TRY HANG-GLIDING INSTEAD?

YOOK!
OURCH!

SIZZLIN' SKI-BOOTS! WE'RE SLITHERING STRAIGHT TOWARDS THE SKI-LODGE.

INSIDE—
IF KELLY AND CEDRIC DON'T TURN UP SOON, THEY'LL HAVE HAD THEIR CHIPS.
AND THEIR SAUSAGE AND MASH! HO! HO!

CRASH!
GLOOP!
YOW!
ULK!

IT'S THEM—AND THEY'VE KNOCKED THEMSELVES OUT!
CALL AN AMBULANCE.

OW!
DOH!
STEADY, MR KELLY!

LATER—
WE'LL DO NO MORE SKIING, THIS HOLIDAY. LET'S SIT OUTSIDE AND THINK ABOUT THIS YETI MYSTERY.
LE BANK
'ELP! SEND FOR LE POLICE!
IT'S A YETI BANK-JOB THIS TIME. C'MON, CEDRIC.
THEY'VE GOT SKI-BIKES. WE'LL NEVER CATCH THEM.
YETI—WITH SKI-BIKES? QUICK—GRAB THOSE SKIS.
FASTER, CEDRIC!
A LARGE BOULDER. WHICH WAY SHALL WE GO?
TO THE LEFT . . . NO! THE RIGHT!
MAKE YOUR MIND—HUP!
YAHOO!
CRASH!
THE YETI!
OW!
WE'VE GOT THE YETI ROBBERS FOR YOU, INSPECTOR. THEY WERE JUST CROOKS PRETENDING TO BE YETI, ACTUALLY.
POLICE
WELL DONE, MY GOOD FRIEND, MEESTER KELLY!
WHAT AN ABOMINABLE ENDING—IN CLINK!

SOUPER

LOOK OUT! SIDNEY'S HOPELESS ON SKATES.
OO-ER!
WOBBLE!
HE'S RUN INTO THE LONG ARM OF THE LAW!
THE BIG FOOT, RATHER! HEH!

I HOPE SOUPER BOY IS SAFER ON SKATES THAN SIDNEY! OOH!
SCREECH!
SOUPER-ZIP!
WATCH ME TAKE THIS BEND! HEH!

ROAR! YOU'VE JUST PUT A BEND ON THE LAMP-POST!
BEND!
YIKES! DON'T KNOW ME OWN STRENGTH!

TOO RED-HOT!
OOH! ME FEET! ME SKATES!
MELT!

COO! SOUPER BOY'S GOING FLAT OUT NOW!
SMASH!
BLAARGH!
WE'RE CLEAN AWAY! HAR! HAR!

BOY

BAH! THOSE CROOKS I WAS CHASING ARE MAKING A GETAWAY NOW!
HAR! LET'S GO!
ULP! S-SORRY, SIR!

ONE SWIG OF SOUPER SOUP AND IT'S . . .
SOUPER BOY TO THE RESCUE! GLOOP!
POW!
BLAM!
ZAP!
WOBBLE!

HAR!
THERE! IT'S BENT STRAIGHT AGAIN.
LOOK! THE CROOKS ARE GOING OVER THE FLY-OVER!

BUT—
WOW!
SOUPER-SKATE!
HAR! THEY WON'T GET AWAY FROM ME! HOW'S THIS FOR RED-HOT SKATING?

HEH! NOW THE CROOKS' CAR IS FLAT OUT!
YERK!
CRUMP!
YOOF!
YELP!

BLEUCH! THAT'S THE LAST TIME I GET MY SKATES ON!
WRECKED

ALL KINDS OF TOPPER BOOKS
A HIGH-FLYING ONE FOR BALLOONISTS!
ONE FOR ESKIMOS. (FUR LINED!)
ONE TO PLEASE THE POLICE.
WHAT AN ARRESTING VOLUME!
NEE-NAW!
ONE SPECIALLY FOR READERS WHO LIVE IN AUSTRALIA.
A POSH ONE FOR ART LOVERS.
WHAT ARTISTRY!
A DELIGHT TO THE EYES!
THE TOPPER BOOK 1986

A VERY SPECIAL ONE FOR SECRET AGENTS!
XYB! XYB!
MEANS "HEH! HEH!"
TOP SECRET
TOP SECRET
IN CODE
COME BACK, YOU BOUNDAH!
BOING!
A RUBBER-TIPPED ONE FOR POGO-STICK OWNERS.
BOOGIE!
IS THIS "TOPPER" THE POPS?
A MUSICAL ONE FOR DISCO-DANCERS.
ONE YOU CAN EAT, FOR YOU-KNOW-WHO!
GUZZLE!
BACK, YOU BEAST!
SNARL!
A WILD ONE FOR ANIMAL-TRAINERS.
A GREEN ONE FOR MARTIANS!
GROOBLE-BONK! SPONGLE!
MARTIAN LAUGH
A LUMINOUS ONE FOR NIGHT-TIME READING.
I'LL GIVE THIS GLOWING REPORTS!

MUM'S SNAPSHOTS—

1— DAD AND HORACE ON THE WHIRLYGIG

DAD'S SNAPSHOTS—

1— MUM HAVING A PICNIC

2— MUM ON THE SEAFRONT

HORACE'S SNAPSHOTS

1— MUM AND DAD (AND THE CHIP SHOP)

2— HORACE'S VIEW OF THE BEACH

2— DAD AND HORACE ON THE DODGEMS

3— HORACE'S SANDCASTLE

3— VIEW OF THE BEACH

HOLIDAYMAKER'S PHOTO OF THE FAMILY

TINY
THE WORLD'S BIGGEST DOG!

I'M BORED! HEY—THAT LOOKS FUN! I'LL CHASE A COTTON REEL, LIKE THAT CAT'S DOING.

AHA! THERE'S ONE ON MY MISTRESS'S TABLE.
GEORGE! HAVE YOU MADE THAT CUP OF TEA?

GOT IT! OOPS!
TINY!
BOP!

OWF!
THUMP!

GULP! I'M OFF!
OOF!
CRASH!
WHUMP!

LOOK AT THAT! IT'S MORE MY SIZE!
ROAD CLOSED

LATER—
YES? WHAT CAN I DO FOR YOU?
BAH!

I'LL TELL YOU WHAT YOU CAN DO FOR ME, MATE . . . COLLECT OUR TELEPHONE CABLE! YOUR DOG'S RUN OFF WITH IT!
OOH!

OH, TINY!
WHOOPEE! GREAT FUN, THIS!

Perilous story Number Two—about a bike for you-know-who!

LATER—
POM-POM-POM!

TRING! TRING!
LOOK OUT, DAD!
ERK! SHE'S RIDING A BIKE DOWN THE STAIRS!

I REMEMBER WHEN THIS USED TO BE A COMPLETE BIKE!
TRING!
TRING!
OOH!
BUMP!

STOP IT! YOU'RE MAKING ME REALLY ANGRY, YOU PERIL!
OH, DAD! SURELY NOT?

LATER—
DAD! COULD YOU HELP ME WITH THIS SUM?
HRUMPH! OKAY.

ERK! THE WALLPAPER!
+
+
=
I CAN'T GET THE ANSWER RIGHT!

GRR! GET THAT DRAWING CLEANED OFF THE WALL!
CERTAINLY, DAD!

THEN—
HAVE YOU SEEN MY CADDY-CAR?
NO, DAD—HAVE YOU SEEN MY CLOTHES-AIRER?

BASH! BANG!
BONK! BASH!

HULLO, FOLKS. I'M JUST TRYIN' TO BUILD A BIKE FOR MYSELF.
MY CADDY CAR!
MY CLOTHES-AIRER!

LISTEN, PERIL—STOP DROPPING THOSE HINTS. I'VE GOT THE MESSAGE.
GREAT! ROLL ON, CHRISTMAS!

SO, CHRISTMAS MORNING—
MERRY CHRISTMAS, BERYL! HERE COMES DAD WITH YOUR PRESENT.
HOPING

HERE YOU ARE! ISN'T THIS SUPER? WE KNEW YOU WERE KEEN ON BIKES, SO THIS PICTURE WILL LOOK SMASHING ON YOUR WALL.
AW . . .

. . . ALL THAT HINTING, AND I STILL DIDN'T GET A BIKE.
OH, BERYL . . . A SURPRISE FOR YOU!
GLOOM!

SOON—
YERK! I'M SORRY WE TOOK THE HINT!
YAHOO!
ZOOM!

Mickey
THE
MONKEY

AH! IT'S A NICE DAY FOR A STROLL.

HAH! I SUPPOSE HE THINKS THAT'S FUNNY.
MICKEY THE TWIT MONKEY

YA—BOOO!
HUMPH! HE'S AT IT AGAIN.

BUS STOP
BOO!
RAZZ!
DOWN WITH MICKEY!
THIS IS GETTING WORSE.

GET OUT OF TOWN, YOU MONKEY, YOU!
YEOWCH!
BOOT!

WHOOPS! WHAT NOW?
PETS
TRIP!

HELP!
SSSSCAT!

STAMP OUT MONKEYS
OOO! I'M OFF!

Monkeynuts to Mickey
PAH! THIS IS GETTING BEYOND A JOKE.

ERK!
RAZZ!

GRR! THAT DOES IT! I'VE TAKEN AS MUCH AS I CAN STAND.

THAT ARTIST IS MAKING MY LIFE A MISERY, JUST 'COS WE HAD A LITTLE QUARREL. TAKE THAT, YOU ROTTER.
SLOSH!

GLUB! GRR! COME BACK, YOU HAIRY HORROR! IF YOU THINK TODAY'S BEEN BAD SO FAR, JUST WAIT TILL I CATCH UP WITH YOU!
YEEK!

AH! HERE'S WHAT I NEED FOR A CRAFTY BIT OF ROBBERY—TREACLE!
TREACLE 69P A JAR
SNATCH!

JEWELLE

I'M OFF!
I'LL SOON CATCH YOU, FRED!
SMASH!

OOGH! I'M STUCK!
HAW! HAW! A FLAT FACE FOR A FLAT-FOOT!

I'VE GOT A BETTER IDEA— A TREACLE GU

BANK
OH-OH! A COP! I'LL GIVE 'IM A SQUIRT OF TREACLE.

BZZZZ!
SLURP! TREACLE, LADS!
'ERP! A BACK-FIRE!
SPLUDGE!
CASH

AFTER IT! SLURP!
BZZZZ!
EEK!
CASH

THIS WINDOW IS BRICK-PROOF, SO I'LL HAVE TO USE ME JEMMY ON THE DOOR.

AN' THE TREACLE IS TO GUM UP THE WORKS OF THE BURGLAR ALARM.
JEWELLER

HOI!
YIKES!
WHOSAT?

TREACLE
BANK
THIS IS A STICK-UP!
I'LL STOP 'IM!

HEH! YOU WON'T, 'COS THIS IS A PROPER STICK-UP!
SCOOSH!
BAH!

BZZZZ!

HO! HO! ANOTHER PLAN THAT'S COME UNSTUCK, EH, FRED?

FRED the FLOP

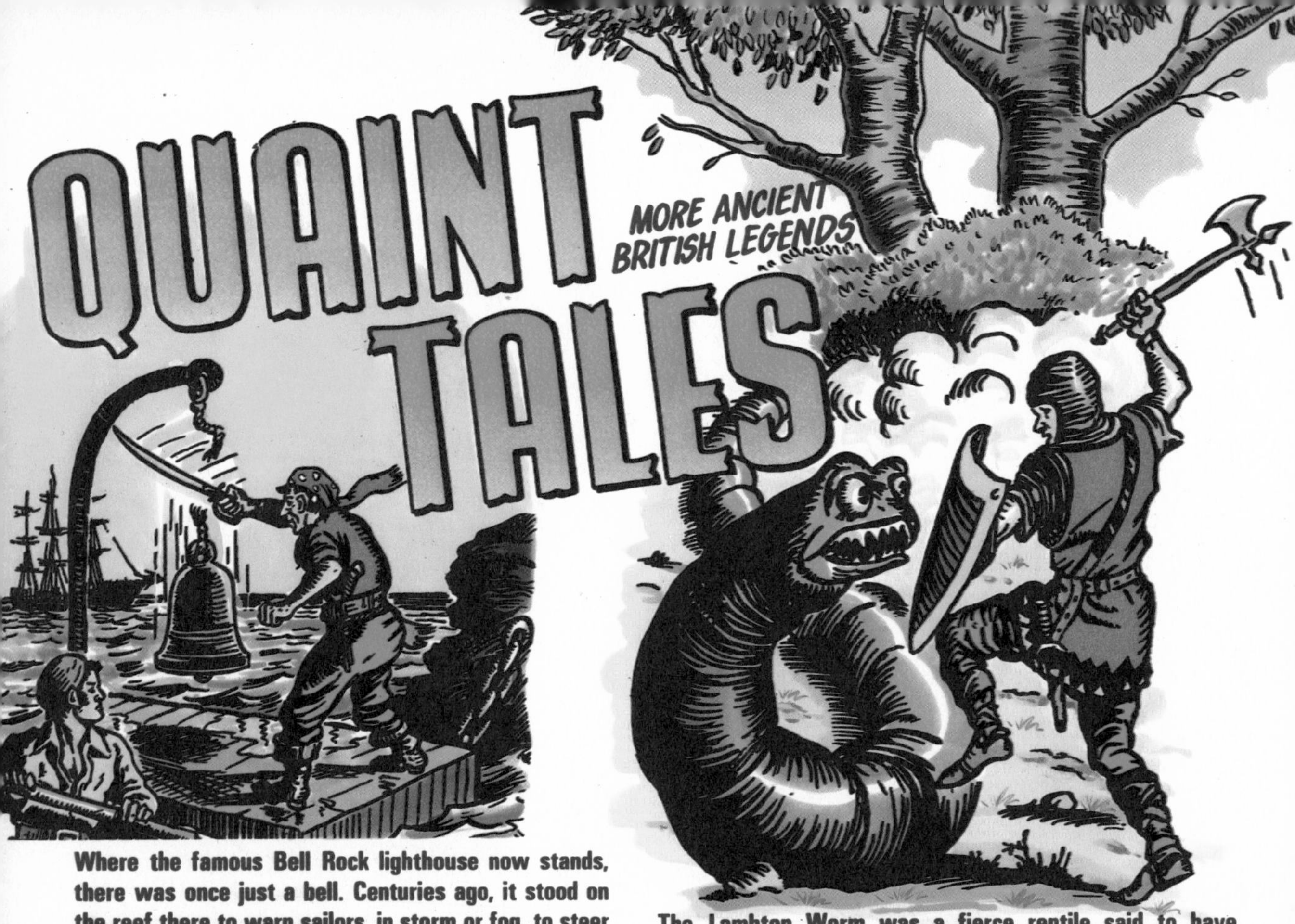

Where the famous Bell Rock lighthouse now stands, there was once just a bell. Centuries ago, it stood on the reef there to warn sailors, in storm or fog, to steer clear. But Ralph the Rover, a pirate, cut down the bell, hoping ships would be wrecked for him to plunder. Later, however, in a thick fog, his own ship struck the reef, and Ralph and his crew drowned.

The Lambton Worm was a fierce reptile said to have terrorised the district of Lambton, in Durham. A young squire, who was determined to kill the beast, was told by a witch how to overcome it, but she also made him promise to kill the first living thing he saw thereafter. He slew the worm, then met his own father. He could not bring himself to fulfil his promise, and as a result a curse lay on his family for nine generations.

According to legend, sunrise on May-morn each year brings out the ancient figure of Irish Chieftain O'Donoghue, riding across the water of Lake Killarney, in full armour! While he gallops, mysterious music can be heard, and it stops again when horse and rider disappear into the mists floating over the lake.

A Lincolnshire doctor, accused of witchcraft, was helped to escape from prison by a shepherd from Wansford Bridge. In return, the doctor told the shepherd to drive his sheep into the church tower next time he saw a silver ring round the moon. The shepherd did so, and very soon after, he spotted a huge tidal wave sweeping towards the town. His sheep were saved, and so were the townsfolk, as he rang the church bell to warn them all.

Peter Thomson, a potter in Richmond, Yorkshire, was out walking one day when he discovered a hidden cave. On entering, he found King Arthur and all his knights fast asleep. Seeing the King's sword hanging on the cave wall, Peter tried to remove the sword from its scabbard. At once, the sleepers began to stir! Terrified, Peter replaced the sword, and the knights fell asleep again. Peter fled, and it is said that Arthur and his knights still slumber there to this day!

The story goes that Ireland was once a land swarming with snakes. But Saint Patrick, the patron saint of Ireland, got rid of them by driving them into a deep pool in the Kerry hills.

On the Isle of Lewis, in the Outer Hebrides of Scotland, the legend of the Blue Men is still remembered. They are said to be weird water-beings who live in the Minch—the stretch of sea separating Lewis from the mainland. The Blue Men lure ships to disaster, sometimes even trying to pull boats beneath the waves.

In old times, in the district of Chatton, Northumberland, it was believed that a ploughman might sometimes be in for an unexpected surprise. Working with what he took to be his own horse, he would be astonished when the horse suddenly shook loose its harness, and flew off! In fact, he would have been tricked by the "dunnie", a magical horse which was said to haunt the area.

Cormoran and Trecrobben, it is said, were two giant cobblers who lived on two neighbouring hilltops in Cornwall. They only had one hammer between them, and they would throw it back and forth as one or the other needed it, all day long!

JIMMY JINX
AND WHAT HE THINKS

POOR DAD LOOKS HOT, JAMES. PERHAPS YOU COULD HELP HIM TO COOL DOWN.
WHEEZE! PANT!
HAH!

I HAVE AN EVEN BETTER IDEA, JIM. WHY DON'T YOU . . . WHISPER . . . WHISPER . . .

GRR! IF I THOUGHT YOU DRENCHED ME ON PURPOSE . . .
NOT AT ALL!

HEY, JIM—YOU COULD ALWAYS USE THAT.
YEAH!

WHAT'S JAMES UP TO?

WHY DON'T YOU COOL DAD DOWN IN A NICE WAY? WITH AN ICE LOLLY FROM THE FREEZER, PERHAPS.

DEFINITELY NOTHING NASTY THIS TIME, DAD. HAVE AN ICE LOLLY.
LOOK OUT, JIMMY!

HEY, DAD—HERE'S SOMETHING TO COOL YOU DOWN.
GASP! WHASSAT?
HEE-HEE!
I MIGHT'VE KNOWN!
SLOOSH!
OOPS! SORRY, DAD. THAT WAS MEANT TO BE A LIGHT SPRAY.
I'LL WAFT COOL AIR ON YOU WITH THIS, DAD.
GARF! GARF! NOT TO MENTION DUST AN' MUCK.
WHOOF!
OH, DEAR! I DIDN'T THINK THERE'D STILL BE EARTH IN THIS OLD SACK.
BAH! I'LL LET YOU OFF THIS TIME—BUT NOTHING ELSE HAD BETTER HAPPEN.
OOPS!
BLEEE!
DROP!
I'LL MANGLE YOU FOR THAT, YOU HORRIBLE LITTLE WORM! GROWL! SNARL!
FASTER, JIM! GOSH! IF DAD WAS AS TIRED AS HE SEEMED TO BE, YOU'D THINK HE WOULD RUN A BIT SLOWER!

TRICKY DICKY
PHONE BOOK

SEE THE SMILE ON MY DIAL? THAT'S 'COS I'M GONNA ENJOY SOME PHONE FUN! A REAL TRICKY NUMBER. HEH!
TRICKSTER AT WORK

TIME FOR MY FIRST HOOT.
TRING-TRING!
WHIRR!
OH! I'D BETTER ANSWER THE PHONE.

HELLO?
AT THE FIRST STROKE IT WILL BE . . .

. . . TIME TO RUN FOR YOUR LIFE!
SPROING!
FLEE!
HEESH! HEESH! HEESH! BRILL!
WAA! SCREECH! HORRORS!

THEN—
COME ON! DON'T DITHER! ANSWER IT.
TRINKLE!
TRINKLE!
DUH! THE PHONE!

ER—YEAH! WOTCHA WANT?
HERE IS THE WEATHER FORECAST FOR TODAY . . .

. . . IT WILL BE VERY WET AND WINDY IN PHONE BOXES!
SLOSH!
YAARGHLE! BLOOSHTY!

SOON—
ARE YOU READY FOR TODAY'S DIAL-A-DISC SPIN?
YEAH! YEAH!

HOWLLLLLL! I FEEL FUNNY!
SPIN!
SPIN!
HAW! HAW! YOU LOOK FUNNY, TOO!

HALLO! HALLO! HALLO! ANYONE THERE? BAH! SPEAK UP! GRR!
BECOMING ANNOYED
HEH! HE'S GONNA GET EVEN ANGRIER.

HE GOT HIS COME-UPPANCE! HOO! HOO!
I SAY! WHAT'S GOING ON? WAARGH!
SPROING!

AHA! HERE COMES KNUCKLES! HE'S ALWAYS LOOKING FOR A FIGHT, AND HE'S GONNA GET ONE.
DRING!
SHADDUP! NOISY PHONE!

IT'S A TELEPHONE BOX, AFTER ALL! HAWR! HAWR!
SHADDUP YOURSELF!
BLATT!
BLAARGH!

OORBLE! I DON'T DINK DAT'S FUDDY!
DING!
DONG!
DONG!
DING!
DING!

'ERE! WOT'S THIS, THEN?
GIGGLE! I'VE SWAPPED RECEIVERS!

HISS!
YERK!
WOW! LOOK AT THE SIZE OF THAT BONE, CHAPS! SLURP!

HOWL! GERROFF, DOGS!
SLOBBER!
LICK!
SLURP!
HAR! HAR! THE DOGGIES SEEM TO LIKE MY TELEBONE GAG!

SOON—

THIS IS MOTORING INFORMATION! PLEASE FASTEN YOUR SEAT BELT . . .
EH? BUT I'M NOT IN A CAR?

. . . WE'RE OFF ON TOUR! STRAIGHT AHEAD IS THE TOWN HALL . . .
YOIKS!
ZOOM!
YEEK! STOP, YOU DAFT BOX!

. . . TURN LEFT FOR A GOOD LOOK AT THE FOUNTAIN!
HEH!
BLUGGLE!
SPLOSH!
ZIP!
SKID!

HAW! HAW! HAW! WHAT A PHONEY PHONE!
GRR! LOOK! IT WAS TRICKY DICKY'S PHONE BOX!
BLOOP!

SNORT! ROAR! SCRAG 'IM!
ERK! I'M OFF!
CLAMBER!

BRR! I'M C- COLD! L- LEMME C- COME D- DOWN!
SHIVER!
GRR! IF YOU DO COME DOWN YOU'D BETTER DIAL 999— FOR AN AMBULANCE!

CUSTARD
GROW!
SPLAT!
HIT ME—NOT THIS. I WANNA WATCH!
SCOOP!
CLICK!